The Wealthy Child: Becoming a Part of the World's Economic Process

by Delvin Sullivan

with Ann Marie Martin

Illustrations by Deno Conerly

The Wealthy Child, Inc.
Huntsville, AL

ISBN 978-0-692-95745-5

Introduction

During my studies and travels while serving in the United States Army, I learned that 7 of 10 Americans have less than $1,000 in savings. Over 80% of the crimes committed that lead people to prison are related to money. With this knowledge, I decided to be proactive and develop a program that would introduce children to the world's economic process.

This program is called *The Wealthy Child*. The foundation of this program is built on seven pillars: generating income, budgeting, banking, establishing credit, making purchases (assets), investing, and giving back. If children learn the lessons in this book early on, we can greatly increase financial literacy and decrease prison sentencing amongst youth and adults.

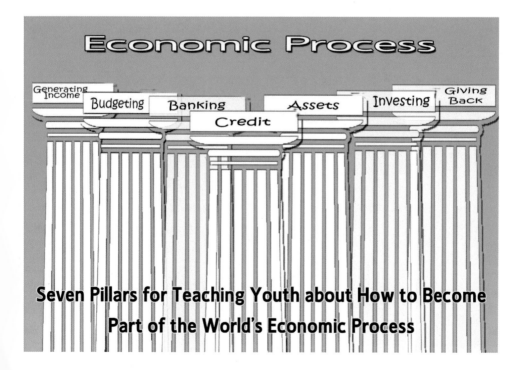

Economic Process

Generating Income | Budgeting | Banking | Credit | Assets | Investing | Giving Back

Seven Pillars for Teaching Youth about How to Become Part of the World's Economic Process

Economic Process

Generating
Income

Pillar 1

Pillar 1
Generate Income: Get a Job or Start a Business

Kamden had wanted a bicycle for as long as he could remember.

"If I had a bike, I could carry more groceries," he told his mother when they walked home from the store.

"I'm sorry, Kamden," his mother replied. "We just can't afford a bike."

Everyone who knew Kamden – especially his best friends, Melissa and Jordan – knew that his number one wish was a shiny new bike.

"If I had a bike, I'd never be late to class again," he told them in the mornings when they walked to school.

Most days, his friends just sighed and nodded. They both wanted bicycles, too. But one day Melissa had a plan.

"I'm going to earn some money and buy my own bike," she said.

"How?" Kamden asked.

"I'm going to get a job. Didn't you see the sign at the Community Center?"

"No," Jordan said. "I was playing basketball, not reading the bulletin board."

"What did it say?" Kamden asked.

"The owner of the best lemonade stand business in the whole city needs two kids to help him sell lemonade this summer," Melissa said. "He's going to hold interviews tomorrow afternoon at the center."

"What if he doesn't pick you?" Jordan asked.

"Oh, he will," she said. "I love lemonade. It's my favorite thing to drink."

"I love lemonade more than you do," Jordan said. "He should pick me."

"It's not just about lemonade," Melissa said. "You have to know how to make a good impression at the interview. My big sister Tierra showed me what to do. She works at the library, and she knows all about interviews."

"Well, tell us!" Kamden said.

"I will. Meet me after school."

*****

That afternoon, Melissa eyed Kamden and Jordan from top to bottom and shook her head.

"You are not dressed to impress," she said. "How did you get so dirty?"

"Playing baseball," Jordan said.

"I slid into home head first," Kamden said. "I was safe!"

"You can't go to an interview with half the infield on your pants," she said, frowning. "That's the first thing my sister told me: Look clean and neat. You don't have to wear your Sunday clothes, but it wouldn't hurt."

"What else did she say?" Kamden asked.

"Firm handshake. Good eye contact," Melissa said. "Let's practice. But don't squeeze my hand too hard!"

*****

The next morning, Kamden dressed for school with more care than usual in a nice shirt and pants. He hoped he wouldn't need a tie to sell lemonade.

All day at school, he couldn't keep his mind off the upcoming interview. Firm handshake. Look him in the eye.

He knew what to do. He just hoped he didn't get nervous and forget. His new bike was at stake!

When Kamden got to the Community Center, he saw a long line of kids waiting outside a closed door. Melissa was close to the front.

"Maybe I should have worn that tie," he thought as he got in line behind Jordan.

The door opened, and a tall, smiling man walked out.

"Good afternoon, children," he said.

"Good afternoon," they chorused.

"I'm Mr. Amir, and I'm the owner of the World's Best Lemonade Company. Who wants to work in my lemonade stands?"

Everyone's hand went up. "Me!" "Me!" "I do!" "Pick me!"

"Calm down, kids," Mr. Amir said. "I'm going to talk to all of you, one at a time. That's how a business owner hires new employees. OK, let's get started."

Melissa was the third person interviewed. She was wearing a broad smile when she came out. She gave Kamden and Jordan a fist bump as she walked by.

One by one, the boys and girls went into the room and came out. Some were smiling. Others looked worried.

"I'm scared," Jordan whispered when it was his turn. He looked even more scared when his interview was over.

Kamden felt sorry for his friend, but there were only two job openings. And he needed that job to get his bike!

The door opened again. Kamden was next. He took a deep breath and stepped inside.

Mr. Amir stood there with his hand outstretched. Kamden took his hand and gave it a firm shake. He was so focused on the handshake that he almost forgot the other rule. Good eye contact! He quickly raised his head and met the tall man's gaze.

"Hello, sir. My name is Kamden."

"Hello, Kamden. Please sit down. Now tell me, why should I hire you to help me sell lemonade?"

"I need a job so I can make money so I can buy a bike."

Mr. Amir laughed. "That's an honest answer. I want my employees to be highly motivated to do a good job, and I guess a new bicycle is as fine a motivation as any. But what about my product? Do you like World's Best Lemonade?"

"Yes, sir. It's really good." Kamden remembered what Melissa had said about praising the product.

"But not as good as a bike?" Mr. Amir added.

"Well…"

Mr. Amir laughed again. "Thank you, Kamden. I'll make a decision in a couple of days."

Two days later, Kamden and his friends were standing outside the Community Center when Mr. Amir drove up in his white SUV. The World's Best Lemonade logo grabbed their attention.

"Hello, Melissa, Jordan, and Kamden," Mr. Amir said. "I have good news for two of you. But before I say which two, I want to tell you that I had a very hard time making a choice. I appreciate your time and interest, but I do need only two employees.

"All three of you came to the interview dressed to make a good first impression. That's very important, no matter what your age.

Also, all three of you gave me a firm handshake. Again, very important."

He paused. "Melissa and Kamden, you did something that Jordan left out. You two made good eye contact while we talked. Jordan, you did not look me in the eye once during our interview."

"I got nervous and forgot," Jordan said.

"Now that you've had some interview experience, I'm sure you'll do better next time," Mr. Amir said. "But I'm going to hire Melissa and Kamden. You'll start next week. Don't be late!"

*****

Kamden made sure he arrived on time for his job. He could already imagine himself riding his new bike – neon yellow with black stripes and a helmet to match.

Selling the World's Best Lemonade turned out to be more fun than Kamden had expected. Mr. Amir and the other employees showed him what to do. At first he asked lots of questions, and they were always eager to help him learn. The best part was serving the customers. Those cold glasses of lemonade put a smile on everybody's face – Kamden's, too.

Kamden noticed that Mr. Amir was always smiling – and always working. He was there when Kamden arrived. He was there when Kamden went home. One day Kamden asked his boss if he lived at the company.

Mr. Amir laughed. "No, Kamden. I go home at the end of the day. But when you are the owner of a company, you are responsible for your company's success."

"That sounds like more work than just selling lemonade," Kamden said. "What all do you have to do?"

"There are three keys to building a successful company," Mr. Amir said. "**Finance** is first. Determine how much money you need to run the business. That includes operating expenses – lemons, sugar, ice, and cups for our lemonade company – plus the salary you pay your employees and yourself.

"**Marketing** is second. When you have a product to sell, you have to generate customers to buy your product."

"Is that why you had us handing out lemonade coupons at the concert in the park?" Kamden asked.

"That's right. It's also why I buy ads in the newspaper. No matter how good our lemonade is, we won't be a success if we don't have enough customers buying our lemonade."

Kamden nodded. This made sense. "What about the other key?"

"Third is **operations**," Mr. Amir said. "That's performing the tasks needed to make our product – squeezing the lemons, mixing the lemon juice with the water and sugar, pouring the lemonade into a cup of ice."

"And serving the lemonade to our customers with a smile," Kamden added.

"Right again, Kamden." Mr. Amir's smile was even wider. "You might make a good business owner yourself some day."

Walking home, Kamden thought about the three keys to running a successful business.

Finance. Marketing. Operations. I could do that. Then I could buy more than a new bike!

Know effective interview techniques:

- Dress to impress.
- Firm handshake.
- Good eye contact.

Three keys to building a successful company:

- Finance
- Marketing
- Operations

NOTES:

Economic Process

Budgeting

Pillar 2

Pillar 2
Budgeting

Kamden enjoyed his job at the World's Best Lemonade Company. He liked his boss. He liked his co-workers. He liked the customers. And he liked the lemonade. But what he liked best was getting paid.

He'd never had so much spending money in his life. He felt rich.

He bought candy and sodas and toys for himself and his friends. He bought a sweet-smelling flower for his mama. He didn't even think about saving money for his new bicycle until his first pay-check was gone.

"What's wrong, Kamden?" Melissa asked him the next day at work.

"I'm broke," he said. "Money sure does disappear fast."

"It can," she said, "if you don't stick to your budget."

"What's a budget?"

"It's a plan for how to spend your money. After Mr. Amir hired us, I sat down that night and made a budget." She pulled a small notebook out of her purse. "See, here is where I write down the amount of money I earn every two weeks. And here are my expenses – including the money I'm saving for my bicycle. If I

follow this plan, I'll have enough money to buy it before the end of the summer."

"That sounds easy," Kamden said. "I can do that."

Mr. Amir overheard them. "Learn good budgeting practices now, kids. It'll pay off later."

"Do you have a budget, Mr. Amir?" Kamden asked.

"Of course I do," he said. "Couldn't run a successful business without one. If I didn't keep track of my gross income, my net income, and my expenses, I'd risk running out of money. Then I wouldn't be able to pay my bills or pay my employees. And I wouldn't be able to build up a cash reserve."

"Gross income?" Kamden frowned. "What's that? And what's net income? I thought all pay was the same."

"I'll explain," Mr. Amir said. "**Gross pay** is the total amount of income that you earn during a particular pay period. As you know, I've set up a biweekly pay period for World's Best Lemonade. Some employers pay on a monthly basis. However, gross pay is not the money you take home. That's **net pay**. It's less than gross pay because the taxes and other withholding amounts have been taken out."

"So," Kamden said, "net pay is what I get to spend."

"Yes," Mr. Amir said, "but don't forget your **expenses**. A good budget sets aside money to live on – food, clothing, transportation, housing. You two are a little young for some of these expenses. However, it's never too early for you to start **building a reserve**."

"I've already started one to buy my bicycle," Melissa said.

"Do you have a reserve, Mr. Amir?" Kamden asked.

"Yes, I do – although I'm not saving for a bike," their boss said with a smile. "I hold back a certain amount of money every month after I've paid my expenses."

"What are you saving it for?" Kamden asked.

"I plan to make some purchases, so some of it will be used to meet expected future payments. But I'm also prepared to handle any emergency needs that arise, like a car repair."

Kamden nodded. Tonight when he got home, he was going to plan his budget – his path to that new bike.

Know your budgeting terms:

- **Gross Pay** – The total amount of income that you earn during a particular pay period. A pay period is determined by your employer but is typically biweekly or monthly. This figure does not factor in tax withholdings.

- **Net Pay** – The amount of income that you actually take home after all withholdings have been applied. It is the amount of money that you take straight to the bank.

- **Expenses** – The money you have to spend to live on, including food, clothing, transportation, housing.

- **Building a Reserve** – Money held back after you have paid your expenses. This money will be used to meet expected future payments and/or emergency needs.

Economic Process

Banking

Pillar 3

Pillar 3
Banking

"Where's my sock?!"

Kamden pulled out each one of his dresser drawers and dumped the contents on his bed. He picked up socks, underwear, and T-shirts, shook them out, and tossed them aside.

"What's going on in here?" his mother asked as she looked at the mess.

"I've lost my purple sock!"

"Why are you so upset? You don't even like that old sock."

"But that's where I hid my bicycle reserve money!"

"Get ready for work," his mother said. "I'll look for the sock. It has to be here somewhere."

Kamden ate his breakfast and brushed his teeth while his mother searched. He was about to leave when she pulled the sock out from under the sofa.

"Here's your bike money," she said. "I'll put it in the top drawer. When you get home, we'll decide on a safer place for it."

Later at work, Kamden told Melissa that he'd almost lost his money.

"You're lucky your mom found it," Melissa said. "I can't believe you put your savings in a sock!"

"Where do you keep your money?" Kamden asked.

"My money is safe in the bank," she replied. "Miss Felichia helped me open my very own savings account. After work, we can get your money, and she'll open an account for you, too."

Kamden had never been to the bank before, and he was a little nervous. But when he and Melissa walked up to Miss Felichia's desk, the banker's warm smile made him feel welcome. She had a good interview handshake, too, he noticed.

"Hello, Melissa," she said. "How may I help you today?"

"Hello, Miss Felichia. This is my friend, Kamden. He wants to deposit his savings in your bank."

"Very nice to meet you, Kamden. What do you know about our banking services?"

"Just what Melissa told me – that a bank's a safe place to put money. Safer than a sock anyway." Kamden placed his purple sock on Miss Felichia's desk.

The banker smiled and nodded.

"Let me explain our various accounts, and then we'll open one that's best for you. Your friend Melissa has a savings account

with our bank. Not only are her deposits safe with us, but her money is also earning **interest**."

"What's interest?" Kamden asked.

"That's the money our financial institution regularly pays our depositors for the privilege of using their money while it's on deposit with us."

"Do you mean you'll pay me to keep my money safe?" Kamden thought this idea was too good to be true.

"Yes," Miss Felichia said. "It's a small amount at first, but it can grow over time."

"A **savings account** sounds good," Kamden said, "but what other kinds of accounts do you have?"

"We also offer **checking accounts**," Miss Felichia said. "Depositors can make withdrawals by writing a check or by using a debit or check card."

"Mr. Amir has a checking account," Melissa said. "I've seen him write checks to pay the man who delivers the lemons."

"I don't need a checking account," Kamden said. "Right now I just want to save my money for a new bike."

"I understand," Miss Felichia said. "Since you're interested in savings accounts, I'll tell you about other options. When you're older and earning more money, you might consider a **money market account**. It's an interest-bearing account that typically pays a higher rate than a regular savings account.

"We also offer **certificates of deposit**, or CDs, which are savings certificates with a fixed maturity date and specified fixed interest rate. CDs can be issued in any denomination as long as you meet minimum investment requirements."

"Wow," Kamden said. "I thought saving money just meant not spending it."

"There are many ways we can help you manage your money," Miss Felichia said. "But today let's get started by opening your savings account."

Know your banking terms:

- **Interest** – Money paid regularly at a particular rate for the use of the money lent, or for delaying the repayment of a debt.

- **Checking Account** – A deposit account held at a financial institution that allows withdrawals and deposits. Withdrawals can be made with checks or by using a debit or check card.

- **Savings Account** – A bank account that earns interest on deposits.

- **Money Market Account** – An interest-bearing account that typically pays a higher interest rate than a savings account.

- **Certificates of Deposit** – A certificate of deposit (CD) is a savings certificate with a fixed maturity date and specified fixed interest rate. It can be issued in any denomination aside from minimum investment requirements.

Economic Process

Credit

Pillar 4

Pillar 4
Establishing Good Credit

Kamden was proud of his savings account. Every payday, he went to the bank and made a deposit. Because he had a good budget, he kept track of the amount he could afford to save for his bike. Little by little, his savings account grew. Meanwhile, he learned everything he could about various bicycle makers.

"I've studied the specs on five different bikes from three different companies," he told Mr. Amir one morning. "I work hard for my money, and I want to be sure I get the best bike I can afford."

Mr. Amir nodded. "You're doing your homework. That's the smart way to make any financial decision. So, which bicycle company is going to get your business?"

"Wheeled Lightning," Kamden said. "It makes the best road bikes *and* the best racing bikes. But those are really expensive. I'll have to save a lot more money before I can afford a racing model."

Then Melissa surprised them when she rode up on her brand new bicycle. Kamden really wished he had started saving his money earlier.

"That's a beautiful bike, Melissa," Mr. Amir said.

"Thank you," she said. "Purple and pink are my favorite colors.

It's fast, too. I'm going to enter the bicycle race this weekend at the park."

Mr. Amir noticed that Kamden looked sad. "How are you coming with your savings?" he asked him.

"I'm getting close," Kamden said, "but I won't have enough to buy my bike before this weekend. Saving money sure does take a long time."

Then Kamden remembered that Mr. Amir had recently bought a new truck. "How long did it take you to save the money for your truck, sir?"

"Not as long as you might think," Mr. Amir said. "I didn't have to save the whole purchase price. I've established good credit, so I was able to finance the vehicle. I'll pay it off over time."

"What's good credit?" Kamden asked. "How do I get it?"

"Pay your bills on time, and don't take on too much debt," Mr. Amir said. "Eventually, you'll establish a high credit score."

"Score?" Kamden asked. "Like in a baseball game?"

Mr. Amir laughed.

"Not exactly," he said. "**Credit bureaus** are companies that collect information related to the credit ratings of individuals. They make that information available to credit card companies and financial institutions such as banks and credit unions. The three main credit bureaus are Equifax, Transunion, and Experian.

"When I decided to buy my truck, I checked my **FICO score** with the credit bureaus. A FICO score is a type of credit score created by the Fair Isaac Company. Lenders use borrowers' FICO scores along with other information on their credit reports to assess credit risk and determine whether to extend credit. The FICO score also figures into the rate of interest the lenders charge. Generally, the higher your score, the lower the interest rate."

"I guess I can't establish a FICO score before this weekend," Kamden said.

"No," Mr. Amir said. "Good credit has to be part of your long-term financial planning."

"The bank may need a FICO score," Melissa said, "but I don't. I'll lend you the rest of the money. You can get your bike and join me in the race."

"Thanks, Melissa!" Kamden said. "I'll pay you back as soon as I can."

"If you do that every time you borrow money," Mr. Amir said, "you'll have a good FICO credit score some day."

Know your credit terms:

- **Credit Bureaus** – Companies that collect information relating to the credit ratings of individuals and make it available to credit card companies and financial institutions such as banks and credit unions. The three main credit bureaus are Equifax, Transunion, and Experian.

- **FICO Score** – A FICO score is a type of credit score created by the Fair Isaac Company. Lenders use borrowers' FICO scores along with other information on borrowers' credit reports to assess credit risk and determine whether to extend credit.

Economic Process

Acquiring Assets

Pillar 5

Pillar 5
Acquiring Major Assets

Kamden bought his new bicycle with the money in his savings account plus the money he borrowed from his friend. He added an item to his budget – "Loan from Melissa" – and soon he paid her back.

Mr. Amir's words about establishing good credit, credit bureaus, and FICO scores kept running through his mind. He wanted to learn more about purchasing a really big item like a truck. One day after work, he asked Mr. Amir to tell him more about loans.

"I go to the bank when I need money to buy a car or a house, or if I have to make a major purchase for my business," Mr. Amir said. "A **bank loan** provides medium- or long-term financing, usually for a fixed period, say three, five, or ten years. The bank charges interest on the money I borrow, and the interest rate will determine the repayment amount."

"How does the bank decide on the interest rate?" Kamden asked.

"They look at my **debt-to-income** ratio. That's all of my monthly debt payments divided by my gross monthly income. This number is one way lenders measure my ability to manage the payments I make every month to repay the money I've borrowed. Do you understand?"

"I think so," Kamden said. "If I work hard and save my money and pay my bills, I can go to the bank some day and ask Miss Felichia for a loan."

"That's right," Mr. Amir said. "But if you want to buy a house, you'll need a special kind of loan – a mortgage. That's a legal agreement by which a bank or other creditor lends money at interest in exchange for taking title of the property.

"When you pay off the **mortgage**, you get the title, and the house is all yours."

"Is that how you bought your house?"

Kamden had visited Mr. Amir's home when his boss held a party for the employees of the World's Best Lemonade Company. He really liked the house, especially the game room.

"It sure is," Mr. Amir said. "But before I bought the house, I conducted a successful negotiation."

"What's negotiation have to do with buying a house?" Kamden asked.

"When you're making a large purchase like a car or a home, you'll want to deal or bargain with the seller over the price. Make him an offer, and he might reduce the price. A **negotiation** helps you get the best deal, and it's another good way to manage your money."

Know your financing terms:

- **Debt-to-Income Ratio** – Your debt-to-income ratio is all your monthly debt payments divided by your gross monthly income. This number is one way lenders measure your ability to manage the payments you make every month to repay the money you have borrowed.

- **Bank Loan** – The most common form for borrowing money for personal use (to buy a car) or a business. A bank loan provides medium- or long-term financing, usually for a fixed period (e.g. three, five, or ten years) with interest which will determine the repayment rate.

- **Mortgage** – A legal agreement by which a bank or other creditor lends money (to buy a home) at interest in exchange for taking title of the debtor's property, with the condition that the conveyance of title becomes void upon the payment of the debt.

- **Negotiation** – To deal or bargain with another or others over the price of a car or home or other large item.

NOTES:

Economic Process

Investing

Pillar 6

Pillar 6
Investing

"Good morning, Kamden!" Mr. Amir's smile was even brighter than usual. "Thanks to you – and your enthusiasm for bicycles – I made a nice profit last night while I slept."

"How can you make money while you're sleeping?" Kamden felt confused. "And what did my bike have to do with it? Did you buy a bike, too?"

"No," Mr. Amir said. "I bought a few shares of the bicycle company. After hearing your glowing recommendation of Wheeled Lightning, I did my own research. I think that company is poised for tremendous growth. My stock is already worth more than I paid for it, and I expect to double my investment in about a year."

"So, do you own the bike company now, Mr. Amir?"

"No, I'm just one of many investors," he said. "Sometimes a company raises revenue by selling shares in the ownership of the company. Stock is another name for these shares. It's also called equity.

"Stocks represent a claim on the company's assets and earnings. As you acquire more shares, your ownership stake in the company increases. By investing my money in profitable stocks, my money grows."

This sounded great to Kamden, but he still wasn't sure exactly how it worked. "How do you make money by investing in other companies?"

"Some companies pay dividends to their stockholders based on company profits," Mr. Amir explained. "You can also make money when you buy a stock at a low price and sell it when the price is higher."

Kamden's face lit up. He liked the idea of expanding his small savings account into this world of higher finance. He could already see himself speeding down the road on the fastest bike Wheeled Lightning made.

But Mr. Amir's next words brought him back to reality.

"You can make money through investments, but you can lose money, too. That's why I diversify my investments through **mutual funds**."

"What's a mutual fund?" Kamden was beginning to realize he had a lot to learn before he could take his money to this higher level.

"A mutual fund is an investment vehicle funded by many investors for the purpose of investing in securities such as **stocks**, **bonds**, money market instruments, and similar assets," Mr. Amir said. "It trades in diversified holdings, and it's professionally managed.

"Before you jump into the stock market, you need to know about all of these things. Take bonds, for instance. These are debt investments that are sold typically by a governmental or corporate entity to an investor for a defined period of time at a variable or fixed interest rate. Owners of bonds are debt holders, or creditors, of the issuer."

Kamden was impressed. "Wow, Mr. Amir! It sounds like you've been working really hard to make your money work for you."

"You could say that," his boss agreed. "Over the years, I've carefully invested a portion of my savings in stocks, bonds, and mutual funds. I want to retire some day and enjoy the fruits of my many years of labor. But I don't want my money to run out before I do."

"You're not old enough to retire," Kamden said.

"Not yet," Mr. Amir said with a laugh. "But it's never too early to plan for it. You would do well to start thinking about IRAs."

"What's an IRA?" Kamden asked.

"IRA stands for Individual Retirement Account," Mr. Amir said. "There are two basic kinds. The **traditional IRA** is a tax-deferred retirement savings account. You pay taxes on your money only when you make withdrawals in retirement. When you're just starting out, you might choose a traditional IRA for the tax break.

"Then there's the **Roth IRA**, which allows your money to grow tax-free. You fund a Roth with after-tax dollars. This means you've already paid taxes on the money you put into it. When you withdraw your money at retirement, you don't have to pay taxes on it."

Kamden had a lot to think about when he rode his bike home that day. Working for Mr. Amir was opening his eyes to a whole new economic world, and Kamden wanted to be an active part of it.

Know your investing terms:

- **Stocks** – A stock is a share in the ownership of a company. Stocks represent a claim on the company's assets and earnings. As you acquire more stock, your ownership stake in the company becomes greater. Shares, equity, and stock all mean the same thing.

- **Bonds** – A bond is a debt investment in which an investor loans money to an entity (typically corporate or governmental) which borrows the funds for a defined period of time at a variable or fixed interest rate. Owners of bonds are debt holders, or creditors, of the issuer.

- **Mutual Funds** – A mutual fund is an investment vehicle made up of a pool of funds collected from many investors for the purpose of investing in securities such as stocks, bonds, money market instruments, and similar assets.

- **Traditional Individual Retirement Plan (IRA)** – A traditional IRA is a tax-deferred retirement savings account. You pay taxes on your money only when you make withdrawals in retirement. Traditional IRAs come in two varieties: deductible and nondeductible.

- **Roth IRA** – A Roth IRA is a retirement savings account that allows your money to grow tax-free. You fund a Roth with after-tax dollars, meaning you've already paid taxes on the money you put into it. In return for no up-front tax break, your money grows tax free. When you withdraw your money at retirement, you don't have to pay taxes on it.

Economic Process

Giving
Back

Pillar 7

Pillar 7
Giving Back

"It's party time!" Mr. Amir told Kamden and Melissa when they arrived at work on Friday. "Tomorrow the Community Center will celebrate the start of the new school year, and the World's Best Lemonade Company is joining the fun."

"I bet we'll sell a lot of lemonade," Kamden said.

"No, we won't," Mr. Amir said with a grin. "We're going to give it away – all the lemonade the kids can drink. We're providing snacks, too."

Kamden looked puzzled. "How can you be a successful business owner if you give your products away?"

"Let me explain," Mr. Amir said. "I've worked hard to make my business successful. I've managed my money wisely. I have a nice home and financial security for me and my family. I've planned for the future, too. I'm in good economic shape, but I didn't get here on my own. Now I'm in a position to give something back to the community that's supported me, and it makes me happy to do that."

"Can we help?" Melissa asked. "I'll donate my time to serve refreshments."

"Yeah," Kamden added, "I want to give something to my community, too. If we didn't have the Community Center, I might never have met you, Mr. Amir. Then I wouldn't have gotten a job, and I wouldn't have earned the money to buy my bike."

"Thank you for **volunteering** your time," Mr. Amir said. "I can see both of you becoming **philanthropists** one day."

"What's a philanthropist?" Kamden asked.

"Philanthropists give money to good causes to promote the welfare of others," Mr. Amir explained. "It makes me feel good to share my hard work and good fortune with people who haven't been so fortunate. I can promise you that our day of **community service** will be lots of fun, too."

The next day at the party, Kamden worked harder than he'd ever worked in his whole life. It was a hot, sunny day, and everybody stopped by the table with the big "Free Lemonade" sign. Melissa stayed busy, too. Mr. Amir seemed to be going nonstop, making sure all the kids had plenty to drink and eat. Kamden thought his boss had never looked happier.

"Hey, Kamden!" His friend Jordan walked up to the table. "Pour me a glass of that free lemonade, please."

"Hey, Jordan! Good to see you. Where have you been all summer?"

"I've been staying with my grandparents. And I got a job mowing lawns. I remembered to look people in the eye when I talked to them, and that did the trick."

"Did you make enough to buy a bicycle?" Kamden asked.

"Well, I guess I made enough," Jordan said, "but I spent a lot of it. So, no bike. How about you?"

"Yeah, I bought my bike." Kamden pointed to his shiny yellow and black Wheeled Lightning Road Special. "Don't feel bad, Jordan. I did the same thing you did when I started my job at World's Best Lemonade Company. But Melissa showed me how to budget my income so I could set aside money each payday.

"Then I almost lost my money, and she took me to the bank where this nice lady helped me set up my own savings account."

"Wow!" Jordan said. "I've never been inside a bank. Could you introduce me to that lady?"

"Sure," Kamden said. "But a savings account is just the beginning. I've learned a lot of good financial strategies this summer. Mr. Amir taught me about establishing good credit. I want to go into business for myself someday. I can see it now – Kamden's Racing Bikes. I may need to borrow money to make that happen. Even if I don't start my own business, I'll want to buy a car and a house. Mr. Amir says you've got to have a good credit score to get a mortgage, and you have to know how to negotiate the purchase price."

"I just want to be able to buy a new bike," Jordan said.

"You've got to think farther down the road," Kamden said.

"Working for Mr. Amir has showed me that. He's invested his money in stocks and bonds and mutual funds. He even invested in the company that made my bike. He says his money is working for him while he sleeps. I want my money to do that."

"You've really learned a lot from Mr. Amir," Jordan said.

"I sure have," Kamden said. "I also learned that it's not too early for me to start planning for my retirement."

"Retirement?!" Jordan shook his head.

"Mr. Amir says you have to be financially secure so you can afford to retire," Kamden said. "You don't want to outlive your money. He told me all about IRAs – that's Individual Retirement Accounts."

"That's a lot to think about," Jordan said. "It sounds like hard work."

"Sure, it's hard work, but it's worth it," Kamden said. "That's something else I learned. When you do a good job of managing your money, you can afford to help your neighbors. That's why we're volunteering our time to give out the lemonade and snacks that Mr. Amir donated. Look around. Everybody's smiling. I've had lots of fun on the job, but this is the best day yet."

Know your terms:

- **Volunteer** – A person who freely offers to take part in an enterprise or undertakes a task is called a volunteer.

- **Philanthropist** – A person who has the desire to promote the welfare of others. This desire is expressed especially by a generous donation of money to good causes.

- **Community Service** – Voluntary work intended to help people in a particular area of need.

About The Wealthy Child Non-Profit Organization

Delvin Sullivan, Founder of *The Wealthy Child* nonprofit organization, teaches his financial education program to youth throughout the United States and abroad.

The Wealthy Child is a 501(c)(3) nonprofit organization established and designed to introduce children around the world to the world's economic process through the financial literacy workshop, The Wealthy Child. In addition to offering The Wealthy Child workshop to churches, schools and colleges across the country and abroad, the organization also provides scholarships, prison and college tours, and educational supplies.

To schedule a workshop for your group, please contact Delvin Sullivan, the founder of *The Wealthy Child*, at (256) 468-3227.

For more information visit our web-site: www.thewealthychild.net.

Made in the USA
Columbia, SC
26 May 2022

60974786R00031